Looking after Unaccompanied Asylum-Seeking and Refugee Children

A TRAINING COURSE FOR SOCIAL CARE PROFESSIONALS

Selam Kidane and Penny Amerena

SUPPORTED BY
THE BIG LOTTERY FUND

Published by
British Association for Adoption & Fostering (BAAF)
Skyline House
200 Union Street
London SE1 0LX
www.baaf.org.uk

Charity registration 275689

British Library Cataloguing in Publication Data
A catalogue record for this book is available from the British Library
ISBN 1 903699 69 X

Project management by Shaila Shah, Director of Publications, BAAF
Photographs on cover posed by models. Photography www.johnbirdsall.co.uk
Designed by Andrew Haig & Associates
Printed by The Lavenham Press

BAAF Adoption & Fostering is the leading UK-wide membership organisation
for all those concerned with adoption, fostering and child care issues.

Notes about the authors

Selam Kidane works for BAAF as a Refugee Children Project Consultant.
Previously, she has worked for family service units and outreach work on issues
concerning refugees and mental health. She came to the UK seeking asylum as
an unaccompanied child in the 1980s.

Penny Amerena has a doctorate in Development Studies and more than 15
years' experience working in international development. Her professional roles
have included Head of Publications for VSO. She now works as a freelance
writer and communications consultant for the voluntary sector.

Acknowledgements

Thanks to the following for all their help with this project: Deborah Cullen, Jo
Francis, Alexandra Plumtree and John Simmonds.

All quotations from unaccompanied refugee and asylum-seeking children that
appear in this book are taken from *I did not choose to come here*, written by
Selam Kidane and published by BAAF in 2001.

This publication has been supported by The Big Lottery Fund.

Contents

Introduction for the trainer

THE NEED FOR THIS TRAINING COURSE

Unaccompanied asylum-seeking and refugee children are among the most needy children in the UK today. Social care professionals play a key role in providing the support and protection that enable these children to develop and mature into well-balanced young people. But knowing how to help overcome the children's damaging early experiences presents a challenge. The absence of birth parents to help provide the conditions for recovery complicates that challenge.

Unaccompanied asylum-seeking and refugee children have experienced a deeper level of trauma and difficulty than many children in care:

- they have been separated from their birth parents, families, language, religion, culture and country;
- they may have experienced disturbing circumstances before leaving their home countries, including war, political unrest, torture and other human rights abuses;
- when they arrive in the UK they experience more uncertainty and trauma while their asylum application is assessed by the immigration authorities and while care plans are made for them;
- as they start their new lives in the UK they see negative images of asylum seekers on TV and in the newspapers;
- they may experience racism and xenophobia in their new lives in the UK.

Imagine yourself alone in a foreign country, missing your family, unsure of the language and the complicated asylum process that will determine your future. Thousands of unaccompanied asylum-seeking children are in this situation. It is true that the UK public care system has looked after and supported many of these children over the years. Yet our long experience of doing the job has not, in many cases, been matched by the necessary understanding of the issues or a confident approach to providing appropriate care and support. Many unaccompanied asylum-seeking children find themselves in the hands of care and support services that are ill equipped to cope with the complex needs they have.

Why is there a lack of awareness and such an inconsistent approach across the country to caring for asylum-seeking children? One reason is that the arrival of these children is often seen as a temporary issue, an issue that does not need longer-term planning and investment. Government policy on asylum seekers reinforces this idea, with the continual introduction of measures to reduce the numbers entering the country to a selected few.

But the fact remains that unaccompanied asylum-seeking children in the UK are **children in need**. Under the Children Act 1989 (England and Wales) and the Children (Scotland) Act 1995, children with no one to take parental responsibilities for them are entitled to a full range of services from the local authority. **The local authority is required by law to identify the needs of each unaccompanied asylum-seeking child in their area. Each local authority is also required to provide services to meet those needs.**

This training course is designed to meet the needs of social care professionals, giving them improved understanding of the refugee context and the impact of the children's refugee experiences.

This insight will help prepare professionals to assess the needs of unaccompanied asylum-seeking and refugee children and decide which services these children require.

Aims of this training course

To enable social work professionals to have a greater understanding of:
- the reasons why children become unaccompanied asylum-seeking and refugee children;
- the impact of the "refugee-making process" on unaccompanied asylum-seeking and refugee children;
- the asylum-seeking process for unaccompanied children;
- the legal framework for the care and protection of unaccompanied asylum-seeking and refugee children;
- how to make appropriate assessments of the needs of these children and identify the necessary services;
- the usefulness of building professional networks and partnerships and adopting an active planning approach.

Learning outcomes

By the end of the course the participants will have:
- an improved understanding of the experiences and meaning of being an unaccompanied asylum-seeking and refugee child;
- an improved understanding of the UK asylum-seeking process and the legal framework for the care and protection of unaccompanied asylum-seeking and refugee children;
- an increased awareness of the needs of unaccompanied asylum-seeking and refugee children;
- an improved awareness to meet the needs of unaccompanied asylum-seeking and refugee children;
- started to identify networks of support and forms of professional partnership, as well as beginning to form an action plan.

Who this course is for

The course is designed as introductory training for multidisciplinary teams of social work professionals from:
- the same organisation;

or
- different agencies with similar training needs.

The approach of the course

The course puts strong emphasis on building on participants' existing knowledge. This know-how might have been gained through working directly with unaccompanied asylum-seeking children or working with other children in need. The course encourages participants to use their own experiences to help them gain insight into the experiences of unaccompanied children. The sessions cover key themes directly addressing the aims of the course set out above.

Size of the course

We recommend that this course is delivered to groups of between eight and sixteen participants.

Length and structure of the training course

This course is intended to run over **one day** or could run over **two half days**.

It is impossible to cover all the information for social care professionals working with unaccompanied asylum-seeking and refugee children in an introductory course. We have, therefore, selected key topics for this introductory exploration. The first three sessions cover topics that aim to improve participants' understanding of the range of issues relating to the children's experiences and the asylum-seeking process. The final two sessions cover topics that aim to build the social workers' understanding of the needs of the children and the planning of appropriate services.

The course can be delivered in 7 hours. We recommend you add 1 hour and 30 minutes for morning, midday and afternoon breaks so that participants can re-energise. The Course Outline presented in Session 1 guides you on how to organise the day. Using the suggested timing you could, for example, start the course at 9am and finish before 6pm. It will be important to keep to time within sessions to ensure all the material is covered well. (See Guidance for trainers below.) You might also emphasise to participants the need to arrive on time for registration so you can get off to a good start.

To get the best from this course

Agencies should ensure that trainers have:
- a relevant social work background and that they are familiar with the issues involved in caring for unaccompanied asylum-seeking and refugee children;*
- basic training skills;
- a commitment to anti-discriminatory practice;
- the time to become familiar with the course content and confident in delivering it.

*Where this is not the case, it is recommended that agencies seek expert advice from BAAF or similar organisations.

Practical preparation for the course

Welcome: as participants arrive, offer them tea, coffee or other drinks, give each of them a name badge and explain where toilets and fire exits are.

Materials and equipment: for every session you will need:
- a flipchart, marker pens and sticky tack;
- an overhead projector and screen;
- a laptop computer;
- pens for participants;
- name badges for the trainer and participants.

Throughout this Trainer's Guide we also give you a list of the additional materials required for each session.

CD-ROM – overheads and handouts

Please note that all overheads and handouts for this course are provided in two pdf files on the CD-ROM on the inside back cover. You will need to print these off for the course, and instructions are provided on the CD itself. These are read-only files, which means that you will not be able to alter them but can only print them off as provided. All of the overheads are reproduced in whole within the text of this guide, and so are the handouts, many of which replicate the overheads.

Guidance for trainers

Course leaders will have different levels of training experience. To help those trainers with less experience, we provide a **Trainer's introduction** and **Trainer's preparation** at the beginning of each session. These summarise the number and type of presentations and activities included (for example, overhead presentations, flipchart activity, practical exercises), a list of specific materials and resources needed for each session, plus guidance on timing.

Throughout we provide guidance on how to encourage discussion and the key points the group should cover.

Finally, here are some **Trainer's tips** to remind you of a few practical points we can all sometimes forget as we concentrate on delivering the content of the session.

- **Overheads:** A good way to encourage participants to focus on what you are saying, rather than reading the rest of the overhead, is to cover up all the bullet points, below the one you are discussing, with a blank sheet of paper. As you finish a bullet point, move the paper down to uncover the next bullet point.

- **Including all participants in discussions:** Some people are more comfortable talking in a group than others. If you notice some people tend to stay quiet in a discussion or feedback session, include them by asking them by name whether they have anything to add.

  If you have split the group into pairs for an exercise, go round the group systematically and ask for each pair's feedback. This gives the quieter participants a much better opportunity to have their views heard.

  (Throughout the course we have provided a wide variety of activities and exercises with different ways of breaking down the group. These include open discussions for all the group, dividing into smaller groups and choosing a person to feedback for that group, dividing into pairs and all pairs feeding back, and volunteering responses in feedback sessions.)

- **Running out of time:** If you are running a little over time in a discussion or exercise and you have covered the main points, ask if anyone has anything different to add, instead of going round the group one by one.

  If you are running out of time because of questions from the group, agree with the group that you overrun into the break or lunch or at the end of the day, for five to ten minutes. It is important to give time to answer the group's questions.

  If you are over-running seriously, look at the rest of the session, or sessions coming up. Where sessions include an exercise with three or more case studies, you could drop one. This means the participants will be divided into a smaller number of groups and you will save time on feeding back. You should try to avoid this if at all possible, because it means the group will miss some useful material.

- **Dealing with questions:** You should try to answer all relevant questions. However, if a participant asks very specific questions that do not concern the majority of the group, say that you are getting into an area that is too specific for that session. Tell them that you would be happy to talk it through individually at the break.

Introduction to the course

TRAINER'S INTRODUCTION

Purpose
The purpose of this session is to explain the aims and content of the course and inform participants of the learning outcomes they will have at the end of the course. The session goes on to explore the principles of social work and the relevant child care legislation in England, Wales and Scotland, and encourages participants to recognise the relevance of their existing experience to working with unaccompanied asylum-seeking and refugee children.

Learning outcomes
By the end of this session participants will:
- understand the aims of the course;
- have an overview of the content of the course;
- know the learning outcomes they are working towards;
- understand the ground rules for the course;
- recognise the relevance of their experience to working with unaccompanied asylum-seeking and refugee children.

TRAINER'S PREPARATION

Session activities
This session includes:
  5 overhead presentations
  4 handouts (ensure you have a copy of each handout for each participant)
  1 flipchart activity
  2 practical exercises

Materials
As well as the standard equipment and materials listed on page 4 you will need the following for this session:
  Overhead 1: Aims of the course
  Overhead 2: Course outline
  Overhead 3: Learning outcomes
  Overhead 4: Some key principles of working with unaccompanied refugee children
  Overhead 5: Building on my experience to work with unaccompanied refugee children
  Handout 1: Aims of the course
  Handout 2: Course outline
  Handout 3: Learning outcomes
  Handout 4: Building on my experience to work with unaccompanied refugee children

Session plan

Introductions	**5 minutes**
Aims of the course	**5 minutes**
Course outline	**5 minutes**
Learning outcomes	**5 minutes**
Definitions	**5 minutes**
Ground rules	**5 minutes**
Building on our experience to work with unaccompanied refugee children	**30 minutes**

TRAINER'S GUIDANCE

5 mins

Introductions

Formally welcome participants. Introduce yourself and explain your professional background and its relevance to this course.

Explain to the group that every participant, including you as the trainer, brings with them a set of experiences, knowledge and professional expertise that influence how they see the world. Tell the group that your job as the trainer is to acknowledge the importance of these differences to help create a positive learning environment. Your job is also to encourage all group members to recognise the relevance of their experience and to build on this foundation to help them work effectively with unaccompanied refugee children.

Start at one side of the room and ask participants to introduce themselves in turn, giving their name and role in their organisation and ask them to say what they hope to get out of the course. It is useful to make a quick note of where an individual's needs match the content of a particular session. This will help you highlight specific points of relevance to participants during the day, and help them get the most out of the training.

5 mins

Aims of the course

Display Overhead 1 on the screen

Overhead 1

Aims of the course

To enable social work professionals to have an improved understanding of:
- the reasons why children become unaccompanied asylum-seeking and refugee children;
- the impact of the "refugee-making process" on unaccompanied asylum-seeking and refugee children;
- the asylum-seeking process for unaccompanied children;

- the legal framework for the care and protection of unaccompanied asylum-seeking and refugee children;
- how to make appropriate assessments of the needs of these children and identify the necessary services;
- the usefulness of building professional networks and partnerships and adopting an action planning approach.

Talk through Overhead 1 point by point

Explain for instance that 'the impact of the "refugee-making process"' is a phrase that sums up all the experiences and trauma that children go through, leading up to and following their departure from their families and familiar surroundings.

Acknowledge that participants may feel uncomfortable about gaps in their knowledge. Explain that this is an introductory course designed to fill many of these gaps.

Be ready to answer any questions.

Give each participant Handout 1: Aims of the course

Course outline

5 mins

Display Overhead 2 on the screen

Overhead 2

Course outline: Looking after Unaccompanied Asylum-Seeking and Refugee Children – a training course for social work professionals

Session 1: Introduction to the course (1 hour)
Introductions
Aims of the course
Course outline
Learning outcomes
Definitions
Ground rules
Building on our experience to work with unaccompanied refugee children

Comfort break (5 minutes)

Session 2: Understanding the unaccompanied refugee children context (100 minutes)
Who are unaccompanied asylum-seeking and refugee children?
Why are asylum-seeking and refugee children unaccompanied?
Understanding the experience of unaccompanied refugee children

Refreshment break (15 minutes)

Session 2 continues
What is the legal status of unaccompanied asylum-seeking and refugee children?

Session 3: Understanding the legislation that covers unaccompanied asylum-seeking and refugee children (75 minutes)
What are unaccompanied asylum-seeking refugee children's legal entitlements under the Children Act 1989 (England and Wales) and the Children (Scotland) Act 1995?

Lunch break (50 minutes)

Session 3 continues
What are the key legal responsibilities that local authorities have towards unaccompanied refugee children in England, Wales and Scotland?
What is the key legislation governing unaccompanied asylum-seeking refugee children as they leave care?
Looking at immigration legislation and the social care professional's role
Exploring how well UK legislation and participants' agency policies reflect key principles of United Nations Convention on the Rights of the Child

Comfort break (5 minutes)

Session 4: Assessing unaccompanied asylum-seeking and refugee children's needs and identifying appropriate services (90 minutes)
Assessing the needs of unaccompanied refugee children and identifying appropriate services
Identifying appropriate placements for unaccompanied refugee children
Assessing leaving care needs and identifying appropriate services

Refreshment break (15 minutes)

Session 5: Building professional partnerships, networking and action planning in work with unaccompanied asylum-seeking and refugee children (85 minutes)
Looking at the value of building professional partnerships and networking
An introduction to mapping networks of partnerships and contacts
An introduction to action planning
Closing the course

 Talk through Overhead 2

Tell the participants the course runs for one day. Explain it is an introductory course and cannot cover all aspects of social care for unaccompanied asylum-seeking and refugee children. The course therefore covers selected key topics for this introductory exploration. The first three sessions cover topics that aim to improve participants' understanding of the range of issues relating to the children's experiences and the asylum-seeking process. The final two sessions cover topics that aim to build the social workers' understanding of the needs of the children and the planning of appropriate services.

Say that there is a lot to cover and that participants will notice the day has been divided into manageable chunks with a number of breaks. Tell participants that the comfort breaks allow people to move around and re-energise, or go to the toilet if they wish; they are not refreshment breaks.

Give each participant Handout 2: Course outline

Learning outcomes

5 mins

 Display Overhead 3 on the screen

Overhead 3

Learning outcomes

By the end of the course you will have:
- improved your understanding of the experiences and meaning of being an unaccompanied asylum-seeking or refugee child;
- improved your understanding of the UK asylum-seeking process and the legal framework for the care and protection of unaccompanied asylum-seeking and refugee children;
- increased your awareness of the needs of unaccompanied asylum-seeking and refugee children;
- improved your awareness to meet the needs of unaccompanied asylum-seeking and refugee children;
- started to identify networks of support and forms of professional partnership as well as beginning to form an action plan

 Talk through Overhead 3 point by point

Explain that by the end of the course participants will have received an introduction to the issues, and have improved understanding of how to approach working with unaccompanied children. Be ready to answer any questions.

 Give each participant Handout 3: Learning outcomes

Definitions

Explain that as you go through the course terms like the "asylum-seeking process" and the "refugee-making process" will be defined. At this stage explain that you need to shorten one phrase that participants have heard a number of times already: unaccompanied asylum-seeking and refugee children. Say that for the sake of simplicity you will often refer to all the children as unaccompanied refugee children. Give the group the following working definition of these terms and say a more detailed explanation is given in Session 3.

- **An unaccompanied asylum-seeking child is a child who is separated from both parents and no other primary carer can be identified, and who is seeking refugee status under the terms of the 1951 UN Convention.**
- **An unaccompanied refugee child is a former unaccompanied asylum-seeking child who has been given refugee status by the immigration authorities.**

Ground rules

5 mins

Explain to the group that it is important for you, as the trainer, to create a safe learning environment where group members can discuss issues openly, share ideas and learning, and develop skills. To do this you need to agree a set of ground rules with the group that enables the participants to learn in an atmosphere of respect towards all members of the group. It is important to recognise that ground rules are most likely to be followed if they come from the group.

As social care professionals, the participants are likely to be familiar with this way of working and you may be able to move through this exercise fairly quickly.

Flipchart activity

Use the flipchart to record suggestions from the group.

Look at the list below. You may need to prompt the group if any of these points are left out. Once the group has agreed a list, which includes these points, display this ground rules chart in the training room throughout the course. You may need to write it out again clearly during a break.

Be ready to remind participants of the ground rules they have agreed, or add more rules during the course.

Remember the needs of asylum seekers and refugees is a topic that has caused some extreme and strongly held public opinion. It is important to talk openly about this. Say that as practitioners we need to ensure our approach is based on sound practice, judgement and knowledge. Acknowledge that few of us are free from attitudes that we need to confront. In our work we may face issues that challenge our "comfort zone" or activate our prejudices. As professionals we need to be clearly aware of these possible tendencies and how and where they might influence our practice and decision-making.

It is also important that you create an atmosphere where participants can express their views. They should know that they may be challenged and will have the opportunity to challenge as well. It is essential that you establish the importance of and the conditions for anti-discriminatory practice throughout the course.

The Ground Rules Chart should include these points:

- **Listen to other people and respect their stated opinion**
  (Explain that the group should welcome differences of outlook and opinion as opportunities for learning. Opinions should be respectfully stated and listened to.)
- **Challenge other people's views respectfully**
  (Explain that where people feel they need to challenge a member's view it is important that they are seen to challenge the "views" of the person and not the person themselves.)

- **Ask questions and ask for clarification**
  (Explain that, where participants have questions, they must feel encouraged to ask them even if it appears to upset the timing of the session.)
- **Confidentiality within the sessions**
  (It is important that participants feel able to talk about and reflect on their own experiences and the experiences of children whose stories they know. Remind participants that they are, of course, required to follow their agency's child protection procedures and there is no exception to this. It is also important that all participants respect the need for confidentiality in the group and agree not to share details of issues or people discussed in the group.)
- **Anti-discriminatory practice**
  (Explain that it is vital to recognise and respect differences such as "race", ethnicity, culture, religion, disability, sexuality and gender. The group must work within a framework that promotes equal opportunities for all participants and the people and communities they work for.)

30 mins

Building on our experience to work with unaccompanied refugee children

Introduce this topic by saying that the course takes the approach of recognising the importance and relevance of participants' existing knowledge. The aim of the rest of Session 1 is to explore some key principles of social care and relevant child care legislation (England, Wales and Scotland), and look at how existing know-how can be applied to working with unaccompanied refugee children.

Exercise 1: Looking at the challenges and principle of working with unaccompanied refugee children

   Display Overhead 4 on the screen

Overhead 4

Some key principles of working with unaccompanied refugee children

Unaccompanied children are children first and foremost. The Children Act 1969 requires the welfare of the child to be the paramount consideration when courts are making decisions about children under the Act. A local authority must safeguard and promote the welfare of a child who is in need under section 17.

Every child has their own identity and their own circumstances. These must be taken into account and inform the care plan for that child.

The status and circumstances of the child increase the risk of discriminatory and oppressive practice. Only robust and explicit policy and practice will counter the damaging effects of this.

Adapted from Social Services Inspectorate, Department of Health, *Unaccompanied Asylum-seeking Children Training Pack*, 1995

Although the legal provisions are not the same in Scotland, the same principles should be applied in practice. Explain that these points were first identified in the Department of Health's 1995 practice guide for working with unaccompanied asylum-seeking children. Give the participants a few moments to read the overhead and then ask them to work in pairs for five minutes to discuss these three questions:

- What do these principles mean to you in practice?
- Are any of these principles difficult for you to apply in practice?
- What do you think the consequences are, when these principles are not applied to unaccompanied refugee children?

Ask them to be ready to feed back to the whole group. After five minutes ask for two or three pairs to volunteer to feed back. The following points are some of the difficulties and dilemmas that practitioners may bring up.

- The different, often conflicting, demands of immigration and child care legislation make it difficult to provide an appropriate care package.
- Barriers to uncovering an accurate history for each child make it difficult to address their individual needs.
- Barriers to providing equal opportunities for these children may exist.
- The children may have been given powerful messages about what to say and do, that social care professionals are unaware of.

When rounding up the discussion it is important to emphasise that **the needs of the child come first**. We may not be able to overcome all the difficulties. For example, it may not be possible to piece together an accurate history for a child. But we should remember that the more we are able to gather accurate information and provide an individual care package, the more we are likely to meet the needs of the child.

Exercise 2: Building on my experience to work with unaccompanied refugee children

Explain that this exercise is designed to enable each participant to recognise a foundation that they can build upon to work more effectively with unaccompanied asylum-seeking children.

Display Overhead 5 on the screen

Overhead 5

> **Building on my experience to work with unaccompanied refugee children**
>
> My role and experience of working with unaccompanied asylum-seeking children is:
>
> _____
>
> _____
>
> Or
>
> I can build upon my relevant experience as a practitioner such as:
>
> _____
>
> _____

My organisation has the following policies and practices, which may help in providing services for unaccompanied asylum-seeking children: My main concerns about working with unaccompanied asylum-seeking children are:

_____

_____

The key outcomes I want from this course are:

_____

_____

_____

Tell the participants that they will be given five minutes to complete the exercise. If they have not worked directly with unaccompanied refugee children, ask them to think of what might be relevant from their experiences of working with children in need or looked after children, to put in the first square.

Say that after the five minutes they will be asked to explain their comments to a partner for five minutes. The feedback to the main group will take the form of the trainer selecting two or three people to share their partner's comments with the whole group.

Give each participant Handout 4: Building on my experience to work with unaccompanied refugee children

After the participants have had five minutes to complete the exercise, tell them to spend five minutes to discuss it with a partner. Pick two or three representatives to briefly present their partner's comments. This should take no more than five minutes. The main point to bring out is that all the participants will have some foundation to build upon whether or not they have worked with unaccompanied asylum-seeking children before. The course will also give them the opportunity to discuss concerns and work towards the aims they identify in their response to the last statement.

Close the session and tell participants they have a five-minute break to get up, walk around and re-energise before starting the next session

Comfort break (5 minutes)

2 Understanding the unaccompanied refugee children context

Understanding the unaccompanied refugee children context

100 mins

TRAINER'S INTRODUCTION

Purpose
The purpose of this session is to explore the context of unaccompanied refugee children: who they are, the countries they come from, how many come and why these children are unaccompanied. There is also an exploration of the experiences of unaccompanied refugee children. The session provides an overview of the UK asylum-seeking process and possible outcomes of applications for asylum.

Learning outcomes
By the end of this session participants will:
- know the main countries the children come from and have an overview of the ages of the children and the numbers that come;
- understand the types of situations the children are escaping from;
- understand why they are unaccompanied;
- have improved understanding of the experiences of unaccompanied refugee children;
- have an overview of the asylum-seeking process in the UK.

TRAINER'S PREPARATION

Session activities
This session includes:
   7 overhead presentations
   9 handouts (ensure you have a copy of each handout for each participant)
   2 practical exercises (both recording feedback on flipcharts)

Materials
As well as the standard equipment and materials listed on page 4 you will need the following for this session:
   Overhead 6: Let the children speak for themselves
   Overhead 7: Who are unaccompanied asylum-seeking and refugee children?
   Overhead 8: Reasons why unaccompanied refugee children leave their home country
   Overhead 9: Refugee experiences
   Overhead 10: Important legal definitions
   Overhead 11: The legal status given to asylum seekers
   Overhead 12: Some facts and figures about asylum claim outcomes for asylum-seeking children
   Handout 5: Reasons why unaccompanied refugee children leave their home country
   Handout 6: Leaving the country without warning
   Handout 7: What would it feel like to flee your home forever?
   Handout 8: Besnik and Fatmir
   Handout 9: Saadia
   Handout 10: Emilia

Handout 11: Important legal definitions
Handout 12: The legal status given to asylum seekers
Handout 13: Some facts and figures about asylum claim outcomes for asylum-seeking children

Session plan

Who are unaccompanied asylum-seeking and refugee children?	**15 minutes**
Why are asylum-seeking and refugee children unaccompanied?	**10 minutes**
Understanding the experience of unaccompanied refugee children.	**40 minutes**
Refreshment break	**15 minutes**
What is the legal status of unaccompanied asylum-seeking and refugee children?	**20 minutes**

TRAINER'S GUIDANCE

Who are unaccompanied asylum-seeking and refugee children?

15 mins Start the session by asking participants to consider what unaccompanied children say about themselves.

  Display Overhead 6 on the screen

Overhead 6

Let the children speak for themselves

We are young and we cannot go back. It is terrible…really it is very bad.
Mer, a 14-year-old ethnic Albanian boy.

One night they came for my parents. Then we spent many months in hiding. Finally they caught my father and then my brother and I had to leave.
Wellela, 12-year-old Eritrean girl (and her five-year-old brother).

If I had a choice I would choose to stay with my own family and I would choose for no war between Ethiopia and Eritrea. But you don't choose what happens in things like that.
Melake, a 14-year-old boy from Ethiopia.

You could say my country has never been at peace since I was born. So I do not really know any different. I suppose when you come to London and you do not hear gun shots, that can only be good, can't it?
Saadia, a 15-year-old girl from Somalia.

We are homesick and miss our family.
Filmon, a 12-year-old Eritrean boy.

It might be difficult for some people to understand about refugee children. If they want to stay happy, then they do not want to hear our story.
Abdoul, a 15-year-old boy from Somalia.

I was sent because of the war – I did not choose to be a refugee.

Aslem, a 17-year-old young man from Afghanistan, who came to England at the age of 15.

The picture I had was that I would surrender to someone with guns. So you can imagine the misunderstanding at immigration when I kept saying take me to the police so I can surrender. Now I laugh about it, but then I was so scared.

Melake, a 14-year-old boy from Ethiopia.

I want to be with my parents and my family more than anyone else. But it is not as simple as that, and as I am not able to go back to where I want to be, then I want to be happy, safe and successful where I am. I want to get good grades at school, I want to make good friends and get on with my foster family. I want to learn good English and get a job when I am older.

Wellela, 12-year-old Eritrean girl.

Give the group a few minutes to read the quotations and follow this with a brief discussion (allow five minutes). Start the discussion by asking how the children's words have made them feel. Bring out the following points from the discussion: the children do not choose to be refugees, they are separated from their parents and families, and many of them have had dangerous and frightening experiences.

Display Overhead 7 on the screen

Overhead 7

Who are unaccompanied asylum-seeking and refugee children?

In 2002:
- most unaccompanied asylum-seeking and refugee children in the UK came from:
Iraq (21%)
Afghanistan (12%)
Former Republic of Yugoslavia (12%) (for example, ethnic Albanian refugees from Kosovo).
Somalia (6%);
- 6,200 lone children arrived in the UK and claimed asylum;*
- these children were younger than 18. Most unaccompanied refugee children who come to the UK are aged between 13 and 15.

* Home Office estimate

Talk through Overhead 7 point by point

Explain that unaccompanied refugee children generally come from countries that are experiencing civil unrest or those that have recently been, or still are, at war. They tend to be places where minority ethnic groups suffer from religious, ethnic or political persecution.

Ask the group whether the number of unaccompanied refugee children on the overhead is lower or higher than the figure they expected. Comment that the impact of some newspapers headlines and articles often leads us to think the numbers are greater than they actually are.

Explain that to be categorised as a refugee child, the child must be under 18 years old. If a person is 18 or older they are categorised as an adult.

Inform the group that the younger children tend to go to foster homes; 16- and 17-year-olds tend to be supported in various other semi-independent settings. Vulnerable 16- and 17-year-olds may go into foster care. Acknowledge that some of the older children are sometimes put in adult accommodation, which should not happen. In rare cases some older children have been detained in prison, which is against all guidelines.

Be ready to answer questions and to tell participants, if relevant, that their questions will be covered in much more detail in sessions later on in the course.

Why are asylum-seeking and refugee children unaccompanied?

10 mins   Start this topic by reflecting on the relative freedoms that we enjoy in the UK. We have the right, for example, to observe a religion of our choice and to vote. Many countries around the world are at war or have oppressive regimes. Explain that in countries where war, civil unrest, ethnic, religious or political oppression exist, parents strive to get their children out of danger. If the parents are dead, families of the children may try to help. Often people pay large sums of money to agents to send their children to another country where they think they will be safe and have better opportunities in life. In some cases the children escape by themselves.

Display Overhead 8 on the screen

Overhead 8

Reasons why unaccompanied refugee children leave their home country

- They are in danger of being murdered or imprisoned.
- Their parents or guardians have "disappeared".
- They are in danger of being forced to join an army or other fighting unit.
- They are prevented from practising the religion they choose.
- They are forced to practice a religion or take part in religious rituals and activities.
- They are intimidated or tortured to give information.
- They are banned from political activity they choose.
- They are forced to take part in political activity they do not choose.
- They belong to a persecuted social, religious, ethnic or political group.

Talk through Overhead 8 point by point

A key point to bring out is that in the UK asylum process each child must be able to give a clear reason for not being sent back to their country of origin. They must be able to provide evidence of a well-founded fear of persecution in their home country. Children who are feeling frightened and isolated, and unclear about the asylum process, sometimes try to make their story fit what they believe to meet the requirements of the immigration authorities. Made-up accounts of who they are and their experiences can be very damaging to their sense of self-esteem and identity and may seriously impede the resolution of their application.

Be ready to answer questions.

Give each participant Handout 5: Reasons why unaccompanied refugee children leave their home country

Understanding the experiences of unaccompanied refugee children

40 mins Start the topic by explaining that, in order to provide the right care services, we need to understand the refugee experience. Say we have seen that the children might be escaping from danger and persecution. They will miss their families, their home, their country, language and culture. The exercises for this topic are designed to enable participants to identify with feelings connected with loss and separation and relate these to the experiences of newly arrived unaccompanied refugee children.

It is particularly important to understand the comfort provided by the idea of "home". Wherever it is and however difficult life might be there, many people find the loss of home difficult to deal with. Emphasise that although unaccompanied refugee children arriving in the UK might have fled very different circumstances, they all have one common experience: the loss of home and all it means.

Display Overhead 9 on the screen

Overhead 9

Refugee experiences

…the wonder is what you can make a paradise out of…I grew up in a lumpen apartment in Cracow, squeezed into three rudimentary rooms with four people, surrounded by squabble, dark political rumblings, memories of wartime suffering, and daily struggle for existence. And yet when it came time to leave, I, too, felt I was being pushed out of the happy, safe enclosures of Eden.

Eva Hoffman (1998) *Lost in Translation*, Vintage

I am sure the man did not tell the people who paid him for our trip (paid by selling virtually everything my parents owned) that he would abandon us outside the Eritrean community centre once we got to London…When we got to where he was taking us, he told us to wait until we see some Eritrean people, and tell them that we are Eritreans and we want to be refugees. I started to cry and my brother cried too so the man said he will go and buy us drinks…I never thought he wouldn't come back. We left our photo album in his place, and a little handbag that used to be my mother's was the only thing I had brought with me.

Wellela, a 12-year-old Eritrean girl, who arrived in the UK aged 11 with her brother aged four. Their parents had been deported from Ethiopia.

Ask participants to spend a few moments to read the overhead and reflect individually, before you introduce the practical exercises.

Exercise 1: Leaving the country without warning

Explain that this exercise is divided into two parts. Part 1 is individual work and for Part 2 participants will be split into pairs or small groups.

Part 1

Ask the group to work individually for five minutes. Give each participant the following handout and ask them to think about the two questions, note down some brief answers and be ready to feed back to the group as a whole.

Handout 6

Leaving the country without warning

Imagine that you suddenly and unexpectedly have to flee your home because it is no longer safe for you to live there. You have one day to prepare for your departure. No members of your immediate family can come with you.

- What are the things of value that you would take with you?
- What things of value would you leave behind?

After five minutes ask the group to feed back and record the responses on a flipchart. Summarise how difficult it would be to choose what to take and what to leave behind. Ensure that the group has considered the difference between monetary value and emotional value: e.g., how difficult it would be to leave your loved ones behind. Allow 5 minutes for feedback.

Part 2

Next give each participant a copy of Handout 7 and ask them to work in pairs or small groups for five minutes to consider the following questions. Tell them you will select three pairs or groups to feed back to the whole group.

Handout 7

What would it feel like to flee your home forever?

What would you find most difficult?
What would you miss the most?
What would you be hoping for?
Now imagine what this experience would be like if you were a child under the age of 18.

After five minutes pick representatives for three pairs or subgroups to feedback. **Record their responses on a flipchart.**

Summarise the discussion. Point out the difference between the urgency of the practical arrangements and the mix of feelings, both immediate and longer term, that the situation would provoke. Ensure the discussion covers feelings like fear about safety and the anxiety of going into an unknown situation. Allow 10 minutes.

Finally, finish this exercise by allowing five minutes for an open discussion on what this experience might be like if you were a child under the age of 18. **Record their views on a flipchart.**

Introduce the next exercise. This is designed to improve understanding of unaccompanied refugee children's needs and the practical responses participants would make as social care professionals.

Exercise 2: Understanding the needs of unaccompanied refugee children

Divide the group into three smaller groups and give each group copies of one of the handouts below. Ask them to put themselves in the place of the social worker for the child or children in the case study. They should discuss the children's needs and the services they would require and then answer the three questions. Give them 10 minutes and then ask them to choose one person to feed back to the larger group.

Handout 8: Besnik and Fatmir

Besnik (15) has just arrived in the UK with his cousin Fatmir (14). In Kosovo the boys came back from school one day and found that their town had been burnt down and everyone had either fled or been killed or taken away. They could not find any of their family and are not sure what happened to them.

Your local authority has responsibility for these two boys as they do not have anyone with parental responsibility for them. You are beginning to map out a care plan for them. They are ethnic Albanians and speak very little English.

What do you think are the most important issues for Besnik and Fatmir?
What services do you think are required to meet their needs?
What is your role as social worker likely to be?

Handout 9: Saadia

Saadia (14) is from Somalia and has been in the UK for two years. In Somalia, a distant relative looked her after from the age of about eight. While she lived in Somalia, she always helped care for other children and did house work. When her relative left Somalia, she took Saadia with her. Saadia has never been to school until she came to the UK at the age of 12. Over the last two years Saadia has been attending school on and off but found it difficult to integrate, given the gap in her education and the ongoing responsibility she is expected to take at home. There have been issues of inattendance that social services attempted to address without much success. Her relationship with her relatives broke down and now Saadia is in the care of social services.

What do you think are the most important issues for Saadia?
What services do you think are required to meet her needs?
What is your role as social worker likely to be?

Handout 10: Emilia

Emilia (15) arrived in the UK from Angola less than a week ago. She is 12 weeks pregnant. She hasn't said much about her pregnancy, but she might have been raped. The local authority needs to find a suitable foster home for her. Emilia's parents are both dead following a mining accident that claimed the lives and the livelihood of several members of her large extended family. She lived with an uncle before coming to the UK. Her family were members of a minority political group who were being persecuted.

What do you think are the most important issues for Emilia?
What services do you think are required to meet her needs?
What is your role as social worker likely to be?

After 10 minutes gather feedback. Ask the representative for each group to read the case study out to the others and answer each of the questions in turn. Allow five minutes for each subgroup. Encourage members of the larger group to comment. **Record their responses on a flipchart.**

The main points to bring out as the groups feed back are that these children each have special needs as well as experiences, as well as the feelings of separation and loss common to unaccompanied refugee children.

Besnik and Fatmir have seen some very disturbing incidents; they have the added trauma that they do not know whether their family is dead or alive, and they have language difficulties.

Saadia has lived without her parents for a long time, her distant relative has chosen not to look after when they arrived in the UK, and she has no experience of school.

Emilia's parents are dead, she has experienced persecution and she might have been raped. She is pregnant.

Each child will need full assessment and a comprehensive care plan that meets local policy and practice protocols. Together you and the group might also suggest the following needs:

Besnik, Fatmir and Emilia might need therapeutic help.

Besnik and Fatmir might need the services of an interpreter.

Saadia will need an assessment of her educational needs.

Emilia will need a health assessment that addresses her general and specific health needs, including referral to an antenatal service.

They might all need to meet other people from their culture who speak their language and follow their religion.

Take a few minutes to draw the main points of the exercise together. Emphasise the key role of the social worker in identifying and assessing the needs and the specialist services these children require so that a long-term care plan can be set up.

Refreshment break

15 mins

Before you break tell participants that you will continue Session 2 after the break by looking at the legal status given to unaccompanied refugee children and how this affects their experience in the UK.

Session 2 continued

What is the legal status of unaccompanied asylum-seeking and refugee children?

20 mins

Introduce this topic by explaining it is important for social workers to have a clear understanding of the legal status of unaccompanied asylum-seeking and refugee children. It is also important to understand that the status they are given will determine both their immediate and their long-term future in the UK. It is therefore a key aspect of understanding the unaccompanied refugee child context.

Start with some legal definitions.

Display Overhead 10 on the screen

Overhead 10

Important legal definitions

- **What is an asylum seeker?**
  An **asylum seeker** is someone who applies to be given **refugee status** under the terms of the 1951 United Nations High Commission for Refugees (UNHCR) Convention.

- **What is an unaccompanied minor?**
  An **unaccompanied minor** is a child 'who is **separated from both parents** and **for whose care no person can be found** who by law or custom has primary responsibility'. 1951 UNHCR Convention

- **What is a refugee?**
  A **refugee** is someone who **leaves or does not return to the country of their nationality** because of 'a **well-founded fear of being persecuted** for reasons of race, religion, nationality, membership of a particular social group, or particular opinion'. 1951 UNHCR Convention

  The 1951 UNHCR Convention relates to the Status of Refugees.

Talk through Overhead 10 point by point

Remind the group that until an individual is given refugee status they are called asylum seekers. In their social care work, participants may deal with both unaccompanied asylum-seeking children and unaccompanied refugee children.

Give each participant Handout 11: Important legal definitions

Tell participants it is essential to have an understanding of the asylum-seeking process. Explain that "asylum-seeking process" means the legal steps that an asylum seeker takes to gain refugee status or gain the right to stay in the UK temporarily. Inform participants that the immigration authorities consider each case separately. There are four types of legal status that an unaccompanied asylum-seeking child can be given.

Display Overhead 11 on the screen

Overhead 11

The legal status given to asylum seekers

In the UK there are 4 types of legal status.
1 They can be given refugee status and allowed to stay. This is known as ILR or Indefinite Leave to Remain.

The following only give a temporary right to stay.
2 They can be allowed to stay if sending them away from the UK would be inhumane or impractical. This is known as ELR or Exceptional Leave to Remain. No refugees have been given this status since 1 April 2003.
3 They can be allowed to stay if they face a real risk of danger or inhumane or degrading treatment if they returned home. This is known as Humanitarian Protection. It is reviewed normally on a three-yearly basis. After applying for two renewals, they can then apply for ILR.

4 They can be allowed to stay if it is impractical for human rights, legal or practical reasons to return them to their own country. This is known as DLR or Discretionary Leave to Remain. It is reviewed normally on a three-yearly basis. After applying for two renewals, they can then apply for ILR.

5 Sometimes DLRs are given for a period of less than three years; for example, where a child has been refused asylum and is nearing their 18th birthday (in less than three years), he/she would be given leave to remain up to their 18th birthday. If the child does not appeal this decision and has not applied for extenuation, on expiry they would be treated as any failed asylum seeker.

Failed asylum seekers can appeal against any of the decisions. Appeal procedures are tightly controlled and complex so appropriate legal advice should be sought at all times.

Go through the points carefully with the group. Explain that each asylum seeker hopes to be given refugee status, which gives the right to stay in the UK indefinitely. The other categories, used since April 2003, only give a temporary right to remain. This means that the case of each asylum seeker must be considered again. This leaves the asylum seeker in a state of uncertainty.

Give each participant Handout 12: The legal status given to asylum seekers

Participants may start to discuss asylum seekers' rights in general and their access to jobs and welfare. Remind the group of the ground rules if necessary. You may need to have the following facts ready:

■ Asylum seekers who are given Humanitarian Protection and DLR status are entitled access to employment and mainstream welfare provisions.

■ Asylum seekers who are given refugee status are entitled access to employment and mainstream welfare provisions.

The main point to bring out is that unaccompanied asylum-seeking and refugee children are entitled to access to health care and education, and older children will be entitled to access to employment and welfare benefits. There is a lot to cover in the course so encourage participants to focus on the rights and needs of children rather than a wider debate on adult asylum seekers.

Display Overhead 12 on the screen

Overhead 12

Some facts and figures about asylum claim outcomes for asylum-seeking children in the UK

In 2002 a total of 6,990 asylum decisions were made:
   89% claimants were aged 17 or younger at the time of the initial asylum decision
      8% were granted ILR
      66% were granted HP status or DLR
      15% were refused asylum or leave to remain;

11% of claimants were 18 or over at the time of the initial asylum decision

0.6% were granted ILR

2.7% were granted ELR

7.7% were refused asylum or leave to remain.

* Home Office estimate

Comment that these children experience years of not knowing what their future will be as their claims are processed. In 2002 more than one child in five was refused either asylum or leave to remain in the UK.

Give each participant Handout 13: Some facts and figures about asylum claim outcomes for asylum-seeking children

Close the session by summarising the main points of the session and emphasising the key role of the social work professional. Link the last part of Session 2 to the first part of Session 3. We suggest you carry straight on with the first topic in Session 3 before you start the midday break. Tell the group that they have looked at how immigration status affects the world of the unaccompanied refugee child in terms of a sense of security and permanence. Say that next you will turn to exploring how the law guides social care professionals to provide care packages for these children.

Understanding the legislation that governs unaccompanied asylum-seeking and refugee children

Every local authority should provide accommodation for any child in need, who appears to them to require accommodation as a result of there being no person with parental responsibility for them.

Section 20 (1)

Every local authority shall provide accommodation for any child in need within their area who has reached the age of 16 and whose welfare is considered to be seriously prejudiced if the authority does not provide him with accommodation.

Section 20 (3)

Overhead 13B

How the Children (Scotland) Act 1995 addresses the needs of unaccompanied asylum seeking and refugee children

Children (Scotland) Act 1995

A local authority shall provide accommodation for any child who, residing or having been found within their area, appears to them to require such provision because –
(a) no-one has parental responsibility for him;
(b) he is lost or abandoned; or
(c) the person who has been caring for him is prevented, whether or not permanently and for whatever reason, from providing him with suitable accommodation or care.

Section 25(1)

This type of care comes about by agreement with parents or carers, or where there is and is no-one to care for the child, not because of an order. Children accommodated under s.25 are 'looked after' by the local authority. The looked after duties apply to these children. The duties are set out in sections 17, 29 and 31 of the Act and the Arrangements to Look After Children (Scotland) Regulations 1996.

Talk through Overhead 13 point by point

Emphasise that local authorities have legal responsibilities to ensure the safety and protection and promote the welfare of unaccompanied refugee children as for any other child.

Give each participant Handout 14 A or B: How the Children Act 1989 (England and Wales) or the Children (Scotland) Act 1995 addresses the needs of unaccompanied asylum-seeking and refugee children

In England, in addition to the handout, inform participants that a recent Local Authority Circular (**LAC (2003)13**) clarifies local authorities' responsibilities in England following amendments to Sections 17 and 22 of the Children Act (1989).

- The circular clearly states that where a child has no one with parental responsibility (as in the case of unaccompanied refugee children), local authorities should presume they fall within the scope of Section 20. This means that, unless a needs assessment indicates a more appropriate response, Section 20 will apply.
- The circular also indicates that while a needs assessment is being carried out, the child will 'be cared for according to Section 17 of the Children Act 1989'.

As you finish this part of the session, tell participants it is time for the midday break and that you will continue Session 3, looking at key aspects of legislation, after lunch. Remind the group to return promptly at the agreed time.

Lunch break

50 mins   **Session 3 continued**

Welcome participants back and say that the first topic to examine is how the law governs these children's entitlements as they leave care.

What is the key legislation governing unaccompanied asylum-seeking refugee children as they leave care?

20 mins

Give participants some background to this topic. Explain that ambiguity about unaccompanied refugee children's entitlements to care in England and Wales has led to local authorities providing care packages largely under Section 17 of the Children Act 1989. This prevented many children from benefiting from the provisions of leaving care services under Section 24 of the same Act.

In 2003 this situation was challenged in court in the *Berhe v London Borough of Hillingdon* [2003] case (EWHC 2075 (admin)). Since this case, local authorities are reviewing their care packages. **This will allow many unaccompanied asylum-seeking and refugee children to benefit from provisions under leaving care legislation.**

Tell the group that so far in the session they have seen that unaccompanied refugee children:
- fully satisfy the criteria for provisions under Section 20 of the Children Act 1989 (England and Wales);

and
- Local Authority Circular (2003) 13 advises local authorities to use Section 20 rather than Section 17 of the Act in all but the most unusual situations, such as a young person refusing to be accommodated.

This means that most unaccompanied refugee children in England and Wales are entitled to the provisions of the Children (Leaving Care) Act 2000.

In Scotland, most unaccompanied refugee children will be entitled to throughcare and aftercare services under:

- The Children (Scotland) Act 1995
- The Regulation of Care Scotland) Act 2001

- The Children (Leaving Care) Act 2000 and
- The Support and Assistance of Young People Leaving Care (Scotland) Regulations 2003.

 Display Overhead 14 on the screen

Overhead 14

The Children (Leaving Care) Act 2000/Scottish provisions

Entitlements under the 2000 Act and the Scottish provisions are:
- a named personal adviser, who meets with and advises the young person regularly;
- a pathway plan setting out plans for the young person's education, training or employment;
- support and assistance for the young person to continue their education, obtain training or enter employment;
- suitable accommodation for the young person.

 Talk through Overhead 14 point by point

Give each participant Handout 15: The Children (Leaving Care) Act 2000/Scottish provisions

Also, work through the following scenarios with participants. They indicate local authorities' responsibilities in a range of circumstances that social workers might come across in their work.

1 Where a young person has been granted Leave to Remain and the Leave to Remain has not expired or where there is an outstanding application for extension, that individual is eligible for welfare benefits. In practice, the local authority may just be responsible for topping up housing benefit contributions to pay rent and assist with additional costs.

2 In those cases where a young person is not eligible for housing benefit or other benefits, the local authority should meet all accommodation and support costs.

3 If a young person reaches the age of 18 and their asylum claim has not been decided, the National Asylum Support Service (NASS) will reimburse the local authority up to a pre-set limit for accommodation and support costs. The local authority is therefore required to meet additional costs, which usually consist of education or training expenses.

4 Where a young person's asylum claim has been denied and their eventual removal from the country is being scheduled, they are eligible for assistance under Section 24 of the Children Act 1989 or the Scottish provisions. This assistance should continue until they are removed, or until they fail to comply with specific removal directions. If the young person fails to comply, assistance may be taken away under the terms of Paragraph 6 of Schedule 3 of the Nationality, Immigration and Asylum Act 2002. However, the local authority should not remove assistance if the young person has no other means of support. This would be in breach of the European Convention on Human Rights.

Bring out the fact that there are a number of checks and balances under national and European law that protect the young people's entitlements.

20 mins

Looking at immigration legislation and the social care professional's role

Remind the group of the definition of a refugee presented in Session 2:

> A **refugee** is someone who **leaves or does not return to the country of their nationality** because of 'a **well-founded fear of being persecuted** for reasons of race, religion, nationality, membership of a particular social group, or particular opinion'. (1951 UNHCR Convention)

Inform participants that all asylum claims made in the UK, including those from unaccompanied children, are assessed against the criteria set out in the 1951 UNHCR Convention relating to the Status of Refugees.

Explain that there has been a recent change in UK law. Until recently a child would not have been interviewed during the asylum process about the facts of their asylum claim if the necessary information could be obtained in writing. However, in the most recent changes to immigration and nationality legislation, the government intends to interview more children. These interviews are intended to be conducted by a specially trained officer in the presence of a parent, guardian, representative or other adult who temporarily takes responsibility for the child. This development has implications for social care professionals who might find themselves taking on this temporary role.

Display Overhead 15 on the screen

Overhead 15

Who supports and represents the unaccompanied child in the asylum-seeking process?

■ **Who advises and represents the unaccompanied asylum-seeking child?**
All unaccompanied children who apply for asylum in the UK are automatically referred to a Panel of Advisers. This Panel is funded by the government and is administered by the Refugee Council. The Panel **advises** the child in their dealings with public bodies while the asylum claim is being considered.

■ **Does the Panel support the child throughout the asylum process?**
No, the Panel has limited capacity. It is rarely able to support a child throughout the whole of the asylum process. When the Panel is unable to assist the child, **social workers** and other adults need to provide support.

■ **What do social workers need to be aware of if they find themselves providing support in a child's asylum claim?**
Social workers should keep up to date with the progress of the child's asylum application and be aware of and liaise, where necessary, with other adults and professionals involved in the child's care.

■ **What happens if the asylum claim is denied?**
Social care professionals need to know that when an unaccompanied child has been refused asylum and has no other claim to remain in the UK, the child should only be

removed if adequate reception arrangements can be made in the country they are going to. If satisfactory reception arrangements cannot be ensured, the child is normally allowed to remain in the UK, outside immigration rules, on compassionate grounds.

 Talk through Overhead 15 point by point

Stress the importance of liaising with professionals and other adults involved in the child's care.

Give each participant Handout 16: Who supports and represents the unaccompanied child in the asylum-seeking process?

What do social care professionals need to know about the status and entitlements of failed asylum-seeking children?

Flipchart activity

As you go through this topic record the key points on a flipchart. (The key points are emboldened in the text to guide you.)

Explain that **when a child's asylum claim fails they are often given Leave to Remain until the age of 18**. This decision is made because it is impossible to ensure the safety of a child when they are deported to another country. They are therefore given permission to remain in the UK while they are children. This usually means that **unless they appeal against the decision or apply for an extension on another ground, the individual would be expected to leave the country at 18**.

Stress to participants that **Leave to Remain until 18 must not be confused with other forms of legal status** given to asylum seekers, which are **based on humanitarian grounds**. These include Humanitarian Protection and Discretionary Leave to Remain.

Explain that the point when the young person turns 18 is very significant. It follows that determining the age of asylum-seeking children becomes very important. For example, when an asylum claim fails, detention might be an issue. It is not normal policy to detain an unaccompanied asylum-seeker who is, or appears to be, under the age of 18. Detention might be considered if there are reasonable grounds for believing that an applicant has reached the age of 18. When there is no documentary proof of age, a doctor's or paediatrician's professional assessment of age is taken into account. Assessment of age can be imprecise and the benefit of the doubt is given in borderline cases.

The status of Leave to Remain may also cause a range of practical difficulties for the child and those involved in their care. For example, there is often confusion over entitlements to housing, education and benefits. **Children with Leave to Remain are no longer asylum seekers**. As young people they are able to claim benefits and/or support under the provisions of Children (Leaving Care) Act 2000 or the Scottish provisions. However, **they would not be entitled to support from the National Asylum Support Service.**

Participants should also know that **unless a deportation order is served** and/or the young person is detained, then **they are in the country legally and are entitled to housing and education.**

When a child leaves care it is often a difficult transition. The problems and complications are increased for children in this Leave to Remain category. The local authority and social services should give particular attention to helping young people through this period of increased uncertainty and anxiety. **Social care professionals should focus their planning on the fact that these children might be returning to their countries of origin in the near future.**

15 mins

Exploring how well UK legislation and participants' agency policies reflect UNCRC key principles

Tell the group that the UN Convention on the Rights of the Child (UNCRC) was unanimously adopted by the United Nations General Assembly on 20 November 1989. It has been ratified by 191 of the world's 193 countries. It is the most widely accepted instrument of international human rights law.

The UK has stated that nothing in the UNCRC may be interpreted as influencing the operation of UK immigration and nationality legislation, which it nevertheless believes is entirely consistent with the UNCRC.

➜ *Display Overhead 16 on the screen*

Overhead 16

Key principles of the UN Convention on the Rights of the Child

- All rights in the Convention apply to all children without discrimination (Article 2).
- The best interests of children must be a primary consideration in all actions concerning them (Article 3).
- Children have the right to life and to maximum survival and development (Article 6).
- Children have the right to express and have their views given due weight according to their age and maturity in all matters that affect them (Article 12).

➜ *Talk through Overhead 16 point by point*

Flipchart activity

Ask participants to spend 10 minutes considering how well:
- their practice,
- their agency's policies, and
- UK legislation

promote these rights for refugee children.

After 10 minutes, ask for different volunteers to feed back on each of the bullet point questions. Record feedback on a flipchart. Allow five minutes for feedback. Encourage each participant to think about this further as they return to their workplaces.

➡️ *Give each participant Handout 17: Key principles of the UN Convention on the Rights of the Child*

➡️ *Close the session and tell participants they have a five-minute break to get up, walk around and re-energise before starting the next session*

🕐 *Comfort break (5 minutes)*

5 mins

4

Assessing unaccompanied asylum-seeking and refugee children's needs and identifying appropriate services

Session 4

Assessing unaccompanied asylum-seeking and refugee children's needs and identifying appropriate services

90 mins

TRAINER'S INTRODUCTION

Purpose
The purpose of this session is to familiarise participants with possible care responses for unaccompanied refugee children. The session looks at assessment issues, placing unaccompanied refugee children appropriately and identifying appropriate leaving care services.

Learning outcomes
By the end of this session participants will be familiar with:
- assessing the needs of unaccompanied refugee children and identifying appropriate services;
- identifying appropriate placements for unaccompanied refugee children;
- assessing leaving care needs and identifying appropriate services.

TRAINER'S PREPARATION

Session activities
This session includes:
  1 overhead presentation
  4 handouts (ensure you have a copy of each handout for each participant)
  2 practical exercises (Exercise 1 records feedback on a flipchart)

Materials
As well as the standard equipment and materials listed on page 4 you will need the following for this session:
  Overhead 17: Some issues you may face when assessing the needs of unaccompanied refugee children
  Handout 18: Besnik and Fatmir
  Handout 19: Saadia
  Handout 20: Emilia
  Handout 21: Key factors for independent living

Session plan
Assessing the needs of unaccompanied refugee children and identifying appropriate services	**35 minutes**
Identifying appropriate placements for unaccompanied refugee children	**15 minutes**
Assessing leaving care needs and identifying appropriate services	**40 minutes**

TRAINER'S GUIDANCE

35 mins

Assessing the needs of unaccompanied refugee children and identifying appropriate services

Start the session by stressing the importance of understanding some key issues in planning appropriate care responses.

Explain that the previous session has shown that the Children Acts for England and Wales and Scotland legislate for the care and protection of these vulnerable children. Careful needs assessment is vital. Point out that the government's Assessment Framework states that unaccompanied asylum-seeking and refugee children belong to a particularly needy group of children. The assessments for these children require special attention. The Assessment Framework also highlights the danger of these children receiving inadequate or inappropriate services because of their unique circumstances. The Assessment Framework is only applicable to England and Wales, although a similar system is being developed in Scotland.

Tell the group that when they assess the needs of unaccompanied refugee children it is important to take a **flexible and creative approach**. This will help them gather the information they need to complete the assessment appropriately. This approach will be particularly important when assessing the effects of wider family factors and the circumstances leading up to these children leaving their country of origin.

Tell participants that, although the details and contexts of the information the children give might seem unfamiliar, all participants will have professional experience they can draw on to help them understand the personal stories the children tell. This effort to understand will enable participants to identify needs and allocate resources more effectively.

Exercise 1: Assessing the needs of asylum-seeking and refugee children

Explain that this exercise is divided into two parts. Part 1 looks at drawing on existing experience to assess needs and identify appropriate services for newly arrived unaccompanied children. Part 2 considers the children's changing needs as they receive decisions on their asylum claims.

Part 1

Display Overhead 17 on the screen

Overhead 17

Some issues you may face when assessing the needs of unaccompanied refugee children

- You need an interpreter to talk with the child.
- The child feels unable to share information about their past with you.
- You can see that the needs of the child will have serious resource implications for your department.

■ You need to ask the child difficult questions about events they may not want to talk about.

Ask the group to split into four smaller groups. Allocate one bullet point to each sub-group to consider. Ask them to spend five minutes discussing what might be the difficulties to overcome for their bullet point, and what professional experience they can draw upon to help them overcome communication barriers with the child.

After five minutes give a representative from each group in turn three minutes to feed back. **Record their responses on a flipchart**. Divide the responses under two headings on the flipchart: "**difficulties**" and "**possible approaches**".

Some circumstances might be new for participants, for example, working with an interpreter. For this issue you could suggest that social workers prepare carefully for the meeting beforehand and put the questions they need to ask in the simplest and shortest form of words. It is better to ask a sequence of short questions than long questions with a number of parts. The interpreter will be more likely to translate your question and the child's answer accurately, rather than unintentionally leaving out information both ways. You can also check information by repeating what you have understood in your own words and asking the interpreter to say it back to the child.

You can ask participants to think back to Session 2 to improve their understanding of information children might feel unable to share and traumatic experiences they might have experienced. This may help them to improve the empathy of their approach, and this warmth and understanding may encourage the child.

It is probable that a number of participants will have experience of domestic placements where children have been reluctant to share information or have experienced traumatic events, or where an individual child's needs will have had serious resource implications. Encourage these participants to share their know-how with the rest of the group.

Part 2

Explain to the group that you are now going to consider children's changing needs when they know the outcomes of their asylum applications.

Tell the group that they will have an open discussion for 15 minutes considering the needs and appropriate services for the following children:

■ an 11-year-old child given **Indefinite Leave to Remain**;
■ a 14-year-old given **Humanitarian Protection** for a limited period of time;
■ a 16-year-old given **Discretionary Leave to Remain** until their 18th birthday.

***Record participants' responses under three headings: ILR, HP, DLR, on the flipchart**

Encourage all group members to participate. Ask them to think how they would prepare a child and plan for each of these outcomes. Bring out the differences between planning to help a child live permanently in the UK and helping a young person face the possibility of returning to their home country.

15 mins

Identifying appropriate placements for unaccompanied refugee children

Start the topic by explaining that unaccompanied asylum-seeking children all experience uncertainty and anxiety as they wait for their immigration status to be settled. Therefore, it is particularly important to make stable care arrangements as quickly as possible after arrival in the UK. If these children start to build appropriate and significant relationships in their new lives soon after they arrive, it will help them begin to recover some of what they have lost in family relationships and friendships.

Talk through the following points with the group. Where it is decided that a child's needs should be met by providing support under Section 17 or 20 of the Children Act 1989 (England and Wales) or Section 25 of the Children (Scotland) Act 1995, then the local authority is responsible for ensuring that the arrangements are made. You may need to refer back to Overhead 13 in Session 3 to remind participants. However, it is sometimes difficult to provide children with a placement that meets all their identified needs. To reduce uncertainty, social care professionals should tell the children what is going to happen to them and why. Children must know the reason for the placement choice and the plans the local authority has made to meet their needs in other ways. Social workers should keep the placement under regular review.

Tell the group that you will have a discussion on placement choices available for unaccompanied asylum-seeking and refugee children.

Allow 10 minutes for the discussion.

Ask participants to consider the following questions. If participants do not have direct experience of placing unaccompanied children, encourage them to think of how their local authority approaches these placements.

- What placement choices are available to unaccompanied children in your area?
- If it is not possible to place a child in a family or care context of the same cultural background, what does your authority do to meet their social and cultural needs?

Summarise the discussion. Bring out the point that practicalities and resource constraints may make matching needs to placement resources difficult. Nonetheless, it is the local authority's responsibility to find the best fit possible.

40 mins

Assessing leaving care needs and identifying appropriate services

Explain to the group that unaccompanied refugee children and young people need to form a base in this country that is secure enough to support them as they make the transition from childhood to adulthood. This means that social care professionals need to arrange access to appropriate services and prepare leaving care packages. Our experience shows that unaccompanied refugee children make a healthier transition into adulthood where good practice has been followed when their care package is arranged. A good practice approach for an unaccompanied refugee child involves reducing anxiety and promoting trust, security and certainty for the child (Kidane, BAAF 2001).

■ What are the key points that social workers might address in constructing a leaving care package? List these.

A good practice approach for an unaccompanied refugee child leaving care involves allowing them to address their past experiences and enabling and equipping them to make a smooth transition into adulthood as contributing members of society. Emphasise that the success of this transition phase depends partly on the quality of the child's care package.

Good childhood care arrangements provide a base of secure, lasting and appropriate relationships that the young person can maintain as they leave care. These attachments should last over time, whether the young person lives locally or not. Where this is achieved, it gives a sense of permanence and security as the young person moves into adulthood, where the links of family and friends from their home country are absent.

Emphasise that these young people therefore need a carefully co-ordinated leaving care service. These services need to be backed by appropriate policies. Without this it is almost impossible to provide the stability and security that is vital for an uprooted young person.

As part of this service, social care professionals need to clearly explain the factors that affect entitlements to services and benefits. They also need to guide the young person on how to access the services they are entitled to.

It is important for participants to know that the following young people are not entitled to benefits:
■ those whose asylum claims remain unresolved;
■ those who are appealing against an asylum claim decision.

Young people in these categories are supported by a system of vouchers and a small amount of cash each. This service is co-ordinated and delivered by the National Asylum Support Service (NASS), a department of the Home Office.

Inform participants that recipients of NASS support in England and Wales are offered accommodation outside the south-east of England. Those asylum seekers who require NASS to provide them with accommodation are usually dispersed on a no-choice basis. An exception to this is children who have been cared for under Section 20 of the Children Act 1989. These children are not dispersed. In the interests of each individual, local authorities should work with NASS to find these young people suitable accommodation locally. Those children who were supported under Section 17 of the Act do not fall into this category and they therefore could be dispersed upon turning 18. Emphasise how this underlines the importance of whether the child is supported under Section 17 or 20 of the Act as covered in Session 3, and the significance of the new guidance for these children to be considered under Section 20.

In Scotland, children who have been looked after under section 25 should not be dispersed.

Exercise 2: Considering leaving care needs for independent living

Introduce the exercise by saying that you will look again at the needs of Besnik and Fatmir, Saadia and Emilia that the group worked with in Session 2, as they prepare to leave care. Ask the group to split into three smaller groups. **Give each member of each group the appropriate handout.** Ask them to discuss the independent living needs of the young people within their group. Also, **give each participant Handout 21: Key factors for independent living**, to guide their thoughts. Ask them to choose one person to feed back to the whole group and to be ready in 10 minutes.

Handout 18: Besnik and Fatmir

Besnik's and Fatmir's story

Besnik arrived in the UK with his cousin Fatmir two years ago. They were 15 and 14 respectively when they arrived in the UK. In Kosovo the boys came back from school one day and found that their town had been burnt down and everyone had either fled or been killed or taken away. They could not find any of their family and are not sure what happened to them. They are ethnic Albanians and speak very little English.

Besnik is now 17 and Fatmir is 16. They have both been granted ELR until their 18th birthday. Both boys have lived together in the same foster placement since arriving in the UK. They have formed good relationships with their foster carers and are studying at the local college. They have managed to build a range of good local friendship networks and also have links with members of their community from Kosovo.

Handout 19: Saadia

Saadia's story

Saadia is from Somalia and has been in the UK for six years. In Somalia, she was looked after by a distant relative from the age of about eight. While she lived in Somalia, she always helped care for other children and did housework. When her relative left Somalia, she took Saadia with her. She lived with this family until she was 14, when her relationship with her relative broke down, and she came into the care of social services. Saadia had never been to school until she came to the UK at the age of 12.

Saadia is now 18. She has been given ELR for four years and is now getting that renewed. She should be granted ILR. She has stayed with the same foster carer since the age of 14. She no longer has a strong relationship with her relatives and has very little contact with her family in Somalia.

Handout 20: Emilia

Emilia's story

Emilia arrived in the UK from Angola two years ago, when she was 15. At the time, she was 12 weeks pregnant. She did not say much about her pregnancy, but she might have been raped. Emilia's parents were both dead, following a mining accident that claimed the lives and the livelihood of several members of her large extended family. She lived with an uncle before coming to the UK. Her family were members of a minority political group who were being persecuted.

Emilia is now 17. She has been looking after her son with a lot of support from her foster carers. She continues to receive intensive psychotherapy. The responsibilities of a young child often seem too much. However, she is very close and caring towards her son.

Handout 21: Key factors for independent living

Key factors for independent living

All these areas need to be considered very carefully to prepare young asylum seekers and refugees to leave care:

- Appropriate housing
- Practical skills
- Physical and mental health
- Education, training and employment
- Maintaining existing relationships and building new ones

Skills and abilities young refugees need for independent living

- Practical skills
- Self-care skills
- Ability to start and keep relationships
- Ability to access services
- Adequate skills and training and/or education for employment and career

Useful services for young people leaving care

- Primary health services (GP, dentist, optician)
- Counselling and therapeutic services
- Career advice services
- Education and training services (including language courses)
- Benefits agencies (including housing and unemployment)

After 10 minutes ask each group to feed back by reading out the case study and summarising the leaving care needs. Allow five minutes for each case study.

Although there is a lot of information that the social worker for each child would normally know and which the groups will not, each group will have the advantage of not having to consider resource constraints, etc. There should be some consideration of each of the young person's needs across the spectrum of practical, emotional, health, and educational needs, and in the context of the asylum application or whatever has happened to them since they have been in the UK.

If the groups found this exercise challenging, acknowledge that we do not know these young people like their foster carer would. But we can see, for example, that Besnik and Fatmir have a housing need and a specific requirement to stay together. They therefore need help to contact the local authority or NASS about housing and housing benefits.

We can guess that Saadia needs legal services to support her asylum application. Her specific need is for help with her ILR claim. She therefore needs to continue her links with her legal representatives and with the Refugee Council.

We can guess that Emilia needs to continue psychotherapy. Her specific need is to continue with the therapist she knows, if possible, and to find out whether her change in circumstances will affect her eligibility for the free service. She therefore needs help to contact the counselling or psychotherapy service.

Close the session by summarising the main points. Emphasise the key linking role of the social care professional in preparing young refugees for independent living as they leave care.

Refreshment break (15 minutes)

Building professional partnerships, networking and action planning in work with unaccompanied asylum-seeking and refugee children

Building professional partnerships, networking and action planning in work with unaccompanied asylum-seeking and refugee children

85 mins

TRAINER'S PREPARATION

Session activities

This session includes

   1 overhead presentation

   4 handouts (ensure you have a copy of each handout for each participant)

   1 flipchart activity

   2 practical exercises (Exercise 1 records information on a flipchart)

Materials

As well as the standard equipment and materials listed on page 4 you will need the following for this session:

   Overhead 18: An action plan for working with unaccompanied asylum-seeking and refugee children

   Handout 22: Mapping networks of useful partnerships and contacts for working with unaccompanied asylum-seeking and refugee children

   Handout 23: An action plan for working with unaccompanied asylum-seeking and refugee children

   Handout 24: Evaluation form for Working with Unaccompanied Asylum-seeking and Refugee Children Training Course

   Handout 25: Useful organisations

Session plan

Looking at the value of building professional partnerships and networking	**10 minutes**
An introduction to mapping networks of partnerships and contacts	**30 minutes**
What next? Putting learning into action	**40 minutes**
Closing the course	**5 minutes**

Session 5

Building professional partnerships, networking and action planning in work with unaccompanied asylum-seeking and refugee children

TRAINER'S GUIDANCE

10 mins

Looking at the value of building professional partnerships and networking

Introduce this topic by stating that it is impossible for one service to meet all the needs of unaccompanied asylum-seeking and refugee children. (In fact, this is true for these children whether they are unaccompanied or with their families in the UK.) It is important that any assessment and care plan for a child draws on the combined resources and responsibilities of these agencies that are responsible for children's services. It is clear that in this area of work that both social care professionals and social services need to develop networks and partnerships.

Introduce a discussion of the importance of building partnerships and networks to work with unaccompanied asylum-seeking and refugee children.

Flipchart activity
The importance of building partnerships and networks to work with unaccompanied asylum-seeking and refugee children.

Ask the group to suggest ways that building partnerships and networks might be useful. Record their answers on the flipchart. Allow 10 minutes for this activity.

Some of the key points to bring out are:
- sharing knowledge and expertise;
- joint training opportunities;
- working in collaboration;
- improving efficient and effective use of resources;
- providing holistic services.

30 mins

An introduction to mapping networks of partnerships and contacts

Introduce this topic as an opportunity to learn a useful method for summarising professional networks. Mapping will give participants a chance to review the useful professional connections they already have and to highlight areas where they need to develop partnerships and links.

Exercise 1: Mapping your network of partnerships and contacts

Ask the group to work individually for five minutes. **Give participants Handout 22: Mapping useful partnerships and contacts for working with unaccompanied asylum-seeking and refugee children**. Tell participants to use the network map to record their contacts with individuals or organisations that are relevant to working with unaccompanied asylum-seeking and refugee children. These can include both informal and formal links. Tell the group they can add more connections than the lines and circles already drawn.

Handout 22

Mapping networks of useful partnerships and contacts for working with unaccompanied asylum-seeking and refugee children

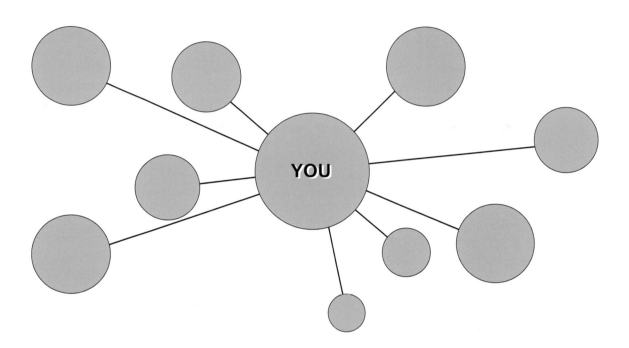

After five minutes divide participants into three smaller groups and ask them to combine their ideas on to one larger map. Ask them to try to group types of contacts together on the map, for example, individuals, organisations, formal contacts and informal contacts. **Give each group flipchart paper to draw their combined map.** Allow 10 minutes for this part of the activity. Inform them that you will need a representative for each group to briefly explain the different types of contacts, partnerships and organisations in their network.

After 10 minutes give each group five minutes to feed back. Encourage participants to make a note of new contacts and ways of working for future reference. Ask participants to inquire about the value of particular contacts they are unfamiliar with.

What next? Putting learning into action

40 mins

Explain to the group that they are nearing the end of the course and this part of the course is designed to give them an opportunity to consolidate their learning and reflect on what they have learnt over the course of the day. An introduction to action learning will allow them to focus aspects of that learning upon specific action points. Say that by the end of the session the aim is for each participant to have identified one or two key areas that they would like to take forwards and develop either for themselves or for their agency. Using the headings on Overhead 18, identify the steps that they might need to take to make this a practical reality.

Explain that action planning is a way of exploring the practicality and resource implications of an action. By approaching a task in this way, the feasibility and the obstacles are highlighted. By thinking about all the aspects of a task before implementation, it is possible to revise and plan the approach so that the action becomes achievable. In the worst case, this approach can show that an action is not feasible, perhaps because of the resources required. But it is better to know this in advance before any resources have been committed, so that an alternative solution can be identified.

Exercise 2: Creating an action plan

Tell participants that they will be given 15 minutes to plan at least one concrete action and preferably two. These should focus on actions that will help them in their work with unaccompanied asylum-seeking and refugee children. When participants have finished, ask for two volunteers to talk through what they have done. This can be followed by a brief general discussion.

 Display Overhead 18 on the screen

Overhead 18

An action plan for working with unaccompanied asylum-seeking and refugee children

Key action	How will it be done?	Who will do it?	By when?	Resources required	Resources available	Obstacles

Go through the table on Overhead 18 and explain the sorts of information that might be put under each heading. You could suggest ideas for actions to start people off. For example, actions might range from participants briefing themselves about refugee children and immigration law, to exploring complex themes of loss and separation. Or participants may choose to focus on the needs and service provision of one unaccompanied child. Alternatively, an action plan might concentrate on a knowledge base that will enable them to work more effectively with a range of unaccompanied children's needs. Another action plan could even be designed to examine a participant's own attitudes to the issues explored today. Allow five minutes for this.

Give each participant Handout 23: An action plan for working with unaccompanied asylum-seeking and refugee children

After 15 minutes ask for two volunteers to talk through their action plans. **Encourage other participants to ask questions and note down alternative ideas of actions and ways to approach an action plan.** Allow five minutes for each action plan. Draw the discussion to a close by pointing out that action plans can be short or long term. They can range from awareness-raising such as self-briefing or training, to more proactive tasks. These might include, for example, reviewing practice and policy of working in the area and identifying gaps in their organisation's policy and practice with the aim of improving services.

Encourage all participants to ensure they keep their action plans and put them into practice as they return to work. Emphasise that this will help them make a start and continue to apply all they have learned on the course.

Closing the course

5 mins

Bring the course to an end by saying that together you have covered a lot of material. Say that you hope the course has increased their understanding of the experiences and background of unaccompanied refugee children as well as how the law affects them and how to assess their care needs. The course has included both information and practical guidance, and hopefully the group feels better prepared to work with these children.

There is much more information available about the experience of refugees, including children, as well as guides which address particular issues. Say that you will give participants a handout to take away with them, which lists useful organisations and website addresses.

A good way to finish is to say you have enjoyed working with them and wish them luck for their future work with unaccompanied refugee children.

Tell them there is one last thing for them to do: **complete an evaluation form**. This is numbered **Handout 24** and is available on the CD-ROM for you to print out.

Say they have five minutes to complete it and hand it in to you before they go.

Session

Building professional partnerships, networking and action planning in work with unaccompanied asylum-seeking and refugee children

Handout 25: Useful organisations

Action for Children in Conflict (AfCiC)

Silver Birch House, Cow Lane Longworth, Abingdon OX13 5EJ
Tel: 01865 821380
www.actionchildren.org
Provides counselling services to refugee children through the school system. Aims to bring educators and mental health professionals together. Project started in London, but is gradually spreading throughout the country.

Asylum Welcome

The Vestry Hall, London Road Mitcham CR4 3UD
Tel: 020 8685 1771
asylumwelcome@mvsc.co.uk
All services are aimed at maintaining the mental well-being of refugees. They run a drop-in centre where they often have psychologists on placement as well as information and advice on many other relevant areas.

Bayswater Family Centre

The Bayswater Centre
14–18 Newton Road
London W2 5LT
Tel: 020 7229 8976
The Family Centre is an NCH project providing an open access service for refugee children and homeless families in the central London area of Bayswater. Services include: drop-in for young children, some under-5s learning provision, advice on benefits, etc., community outreach, counselling and linking people with GPs, dentists, interpreters, etc.

Children's Panel

240–250 Ferndale Road
Brixton
London SW9 8BB
Tel: 020 7346 6700

Ethnic Minorities Law Centre

41 St Vincent Place
Glasgow G1 2ER
Tel: 0141 204 2888
www.emlc.org.uk

Evelyn Oldfield Unit

London Voluntary Resource Centre
356 Holloway Road
London N7 6PA
Tel: 020 7700 0100
www.evelynoldfield.co.uk
administrator@evelynoldfield.co.uk
The unit provides specialist aid and support to refugee community organisations in order to increase their capacity.

Intercultural Refugee Counselling Project

Camden & Islington NHS Trust
Psychology Department A
Archway Campus
Highgate Hill
London N19 5LW
Tel: 020 7530 2350
A counselling service that has two counselling assistants who work specifically with refugees in GP practices where there are large refugee populations. The service is available in various surgeries throughout Islington.

Iranian Association

Palingswick House (Annexe)
241 Kings Street, Hammersmith
London W6 9LP
Tel: 020 8748 6682
info@iranian-association.org.uk
Provides an advice and information service on immigration, housing, welfare benefits, health-related issues, and women's issues. The association has a training centre for IT classes and ESOL classes which are offered at different levels. An Iranian councillor is also available on site.

Islington Somali Community Association

26–38 Queensland Road
London N7 7AJ
Tel: 020 7607 8387
Established as part of Islington's Crisis Intervention Scheme, the worker provides health advocacy in general.

Islington Zairean Refugee Group

86 Durham Road
London N7 7DU
Tel: 020 7561 7480
Offers educational guidance and advice, ESOL lessons for over-18s, employment advice and assistance with job hunting and CV writing. Also provides training in primary health care, hosts health seminars and workshops, mother tongue classes for under-14s and a schools liaison scheme.

Language Line

Swallow House
11–21 Northdown Street
London N1 9BN
Tel: 0800 169 2879
Tel: 020 7520 1400
www.languageline.co.uk

Lambeth Young Refugees Development Project

278–280 South Lambeth Road
London SW8 1UF
Tel: 020 7622 6752
A service run as part of Lambeth Social Services, it undertakes proactive work to help young refugees develop their potential. They are made aware of their rights and groupwork is done to build their self-esteem and confidence.

Assistance is given in educational training, language support, guidance on careers, colleges, the British system generally and helping them settle in the wider community.

Problems resulting from separation from and/or loss of parents, siblings or other family members are also dealt with.

Law Centres Federation

Duchess House
18-19 Warren Street
London W1P 5DB
Tel: 020 7387 8570
www.lawcentres.org.uk

Mapesbury Refugee Clinic for People in Exile

The Minster Centre
17 Mapesbury Road
London NW2 4HU
Tel: 020 8728 2344
www.minstercentre.org.uk
Offers psychosocial counselling for refugees and asylum seekers free of charge. The service is provided by trained refugee counsellors who, between them, speak more than ten languages.

Medical Foundation for the Care of Victims of Torture

111 Isledon Road
London N7 7JW
Tel: 020 7697 7777
www.torturecare.org.uk
Offers social and emotional support to refugees with a history of torture. Long-term counselling is offered through referral, either self or third party. Each case is discussed by a multidisciplinary team in order to provide the most comprehensive support.

Mosaic Centre – Refugee Project and Bosnian Project

145 High Road, Willesden
London NW10 2QJ
Tel: 020 8459 2278
The project is run by Welcare Community Project and consists of advice sessions and group sessions for people from the Bosnian community. Counselling and therapy are provided in non-direct ways such as through play for children, art and drama workshops.

NAFSIYAT

262 Holloway Road
London N7 6NE
Tel: 020 7686 8666
www.nafsiyat.org.uk
Provides one-to-one counselling, therapy and advice for ethnic minorities and refugees by appointment. Its services extend to individuals, families and children. A project has also been established to deal with refugees aged between 12 and 30 years. Referrals are made by teachers, community workers and GPs and a large number of people are self-referrals.

National Association of Citizens Advice Bureaux

Myddleton House
115–123 Pentonville Road
London N1 9LZ
Tel: 020 7833 2181
www.citizensadvice.org.uk

Refugee Action

The Old Fire Station
3rd Floor, 150 Waterloo Road
London SE1 8SD
Tel: 020 7654 7700
www.refugee-action.org.uk

Refugee Advice Centre

702 High Road, Leyton
London E10 6JP
Tel: 020 8558 1865
refugeeadvice@ein.org.uk
Operates a legal advice service, and also offers training, education and employment advice.

Refugee Arrivals Project (RAP)

Head Office
41b Cross Lances Road
Hounslow
Middlesex TW3 2AD
Tel: 020 8607 6888
www.refugee-arrivals.org.uk

also: Room 1116
1st Floor
Queens Building
Heathrow Airport
Hounslow
Middlesex TW6 1ON
Tel: 020 8759 5740

Refugee Children Project

BAAF, Skyline House
200 Union Street
London SE1 OLX
Tel: 020 7593 2000
www.baaf.org.uk

Refugee Council Information Service

Refugee Council
3 Bondway, London SW8 1SJ
Tel: 020 7820 3000
www.refugeecouncil.org.uk

Refugee Health Support Team

2nd Floor
Abbey Medical Centre
2 Harpour Road
Barking IG11 8RG
Tel: 020 8276 7090
The service has a multidisciplinary team which provides transitional care to people who either walk in or who are referred to them. They can provide direct access to GPs as well as conduct outreach work and home visits.

Refugee Outreach Team – Lambeth, Southwark Health Authority

Masters House
Limelight Annexe
4 Dugard Way
Kennington SE11 4TH
Tel: 020 7840 5200
Aims to work with refugees and asylum seekers, improve their access to services and the quality of services offered to them. It has an outreach team, members of which are all refugees, which liaises with GPs, Community Health Care Trusts and others.

Refugee Resource

Hooper House
2nd Floor, 3 Collins Street
Oxford OX4 1XS
Tel: 0845 4580055
info@orsp.fsnet.co.uk
Provides counselling and therapy for refugees, currently limited to the 12–25 age range, although plans to extend the service in the future. Generally third party referral, although will accept self-referral.

Session 5

Building professional partnerships, networking and action planning in work with unaccompanied asylum-seeking and refugee children

Refugee Support Project

Willesden Centre for Psychological Treatment, Willesden Hospital London NW11 7BY

Refugee Support Psychologist – Forest Healthcare

North East London Mental Health Authority
NHS Trust Larkswood Centre
Thorpe Coombe Hospital
714 Forest Road
London E17 3HP
Tel: 020 8520 8971

The service employs a Refugee Support Psychologist who provides counselling and raises awareness among referral agencies. (Self-referrals are not accepted.)

Refugee Therapy Centre

6–9 Manor Gardens
London N7 6LA
Tel: 020 7272 2565
www.refugeetherapy.org.uk

Provides counselling and psychotherapy for refugees and asylum seekers.

Edinburgh Refugee Centre

St George's West
58 Shandwick Place
Edinburgh EH3 4RT
Tel: 0800 085 6087

Scottish Refugee Council

5 Cadogan Square
Glasgow G2 7PH
Tel: 0141 248 9799
Tel: 0800 085 6087
www.scottishrefugeecouncil.(

Scottish Asylum Seekers Consortium

Room 107
Baltic Chambers
50 Wellington Street
Glasgow G2 6Hj
Tel: 0141 248 2396
www.asylumscotland.org.uk

Steels Lane Health Centre

384–398 Commercial Road
London E1 0LR
Tel: 020 7790 7171

Offers counselling to the Somali community in Tower Hamlets. The counsellor runs two groups: one for school-age girls and the other for women.

Somali Mental Health Project

Daryelka Haanka
3 Merchant Street
London E3 4LY
Tel: 020 8980 9797

Provides a range of services to the Somali community, including interpreting, advocacy and support to carers and families.

Somali Welfare Association

Canalside House
383 Ladbroke Grove
London W10 5AA
Tel: 020 8968 1195

Provides information, support counselling and mental health services to the Somali and other relations.

73 Charlotte Street
London W1T 4PL
Tel: 020 7530 3666

This is a service for people with severe traumatic experiences. Counselling is provided through interpreters if necessary.

Traumatic Stress Clinic – Refugee Service

Bicultural Mental Health Service
73 Charlotte Street
London W1T 4PL
Tel: 020 7530 3666

This service is targeted specifically at communities from Bosnia and other areas in former Yugoslavia who have experienced trauma in their home countries.

Traumatic Stress Service

Clare House, St. George's Hospital
Blackshaw Road
London SW17 0QT
Tel: 020 8725 0355

The service's focus is treating victims of violence and preventing the emergence of long-term psychiatric problems.

Young Refugees Mental Health Project

The Michael Rutter Centre for Children & Young People
The Maudsley Hospital
De Crespigny Park
London SE5 8A3
Tel: 020 7919 2534
irene.sclare@slam-tr.nhs.uk

Useful websites for those working with unaccompanied asylum-seeking and refugee children in Scotland.

www.savethechildren.org.uk/caris/ This website provides useful information for children and young people who are asylum seekers or refugees in Scotland. It also provides legal information for parents, lawyers and specialist advisers.

www.scotland.gov.uk/library5/education/syplc-00.asp This is the electronic version of the Scottish Executive's Guidance and Regulations for throughcare and aftercare under the Children (Scotland) Act 1995, etc.

www.scotland.gov.uk/library5/education/pwhb-00.asp This is the electronic version of the Pathways Handbook prepared for the Scottish Executive for planning for aftercare service provision.

BAAF is grateful to The Civis Trust for permission to extract the names and details of some of the organisations that appear in this list from their guide, 'Refugees and Mental Health: A handbook for primary care workers', published in 2004.